—— *the beauty of* ——
DIFFERENCE

J. E. Ayee

Copyright © 2016 Jonathan Ayee

All rights reserved.

ISBN: 0692712585
ISBN-13: 978-0692712580

This book is dedicated to my son or daughter I'll meet later this year.

The Beauty of Difference

Contents

	Acknowledgments	Pg. 3
	Introduction	Pg. 4
1	Who are you?	Pg. 7
2	Early Years	Pg. 10
3	Early Learning	Pg. 13
4	Difference	Pg. 16
5	Better or worse	Pg. 19
6	Becoming Enemies	Pg. 21
7	Difference is okay	Pg. 24
8	Love Training	Pg. 27

Acknowledgments

I thank my parents for valuing education, and sending us to the best schools. I wouldn't have been able to express myself without that. I also owe my gratitude to everyone who's poured their heart and soul out to me even when they knew I didn't see things the way they did. It inspired me to write this book. Finally I owe my life and purpose to my creator who sustains my life.

Introduction

So he said to me, *"You know what? Honestly, I've gotta say I disagree with you, but hey...I don't understand what you're going through, and I'm not going to pretend to either. I just want you to know that you are worth more to me than this... let's go grab a drink, I'm buying."*
– An anonymous true friend

There is something beautiful about difference. Relax and imagine an orchestra playing. You hear strings as you begin to see a beautiful garden. Then you hear the sound of a playful flute, and just like that! It makes you think of a butterfly floating through the garden.

The Beauty of Difference

Beauty is heard in the difference of the sound of the flute as it complements the strings, and brings life to the music and picture.

This happens with people also. We look different and see things differently. And just like the flute and strings, our differences can complement each other and make us come alive.

But this isn't always the case now is it? More often than not, our differences tear us apart, and leave us feeling empty inside.

And why?

I believe the simplest answer is this:

We don't understand difference.

When people are different from us, we typically seek conformity. Either we hope they will conform to our ways, or fear that we will conform to theirs.

At times we feel threatened by them, other times we get jealous, and sometimes we don't even know why we dislike them.

But no matter what we do, *we will always have differences.* And if we have differences, *we will also have conflict.* Let's chew on that once more… and digest it. Okay good.

Conflict happens. What matters is how we handle it. Will we let our negative emotions dictate our words and the course of our actions? Or will we look for another way?

Our differences are like a single spot light shining on a stage where love and hate are on opposite ends.

What will yours shine on?

Chapter One: Who are you?

What gives you a sense of purpose and fulfillment in life? Think it through, and with enough evaluation, you will find that behind your answer is one thing, one word. That word is
…_relationships._

But even though relationships are so important, why do they seem nearly impossible at times? What makes great relationships hard to come by and maintain? It's really quite simple
…_we are different_.

Think about it. At any moment in time we see things from different vantage points that are influenced by the differences we were born with, and the ones that we learned.

The Beauty of Difference

To make this clear, ask yourself who am I? Ask yourself what makes you, you. When you do this, you will come to find that the more answers you give to this question, the more you will see how different you are from everyone else.

Let's get the ball rolling and start with your physical appearance. Are you male or female? Because if you are male, it is likely that in a very general sense, the way you see the world will align more closely with other males, and if you are female, you probably see things as other females do.

What about age? How old are you? Do you spend a lot of time with people who are the same age as you? Again, it's likely that the way you see things aligns more closely to people who are about the same age as you.

What about race and ethnicity? Do you spend most of your time with a particular race or culture? If you do, your cultural views may align more closely with that race or culture.

These are just a few physical things that define people's perception of themselves, and these differences have the ability to shine the spotlight on love or hate.

No matter what your individuality looks like, it is ground breaking to remember that in any relationship, *you are you,* and *they are them.* You don't have to be them, and they don't have to be you.

You are the only you. And there is something amazing in you that the world has got to see. Don't hide it. Show it because people can benefit from it.

**For the next twenty-one days, take a moment to repeat this sentence out loud or in your head. **

"I am the real me, a special gift only I can be."

Chapter Two: Early Years.

Think back to your childhood environment. What do you see, and what do you feel? Do you think it influenced the way you see the world today?

Whenever we disagree with each other, we don't remember the history behind the way we think. And quite often in these moments, we just want to be understood. But that's not always possible, because how we think and feel dates back to events from our early years. And those events aren't easy to remember in the middle of an argument.

If you've ever observed a happy old married couple, you probably noticed that their happiness wasn't dependent on whether they completely understood each other. That is because after many years, they learned that they couldn't ever completely see things from each other's point of view. The love they show to each other is more evident because of their willingness to continue to do so despite being different. The spotlight shines on their love.

Take another moment to think about where you spent your early years. Can you identify the different things that helped shape your thinking? Write them down. Then the next time you have an argument with someone, consider how those things influenced the conversation, while keeping in mind the fact that the other person can't see those things.

It's important to realize that our childhood environment and experiences helped shape us even if we don't remember them vividly. Back then, we absorbed nearly everything we were exposed to because our sense of judgment wasn't quite as developed as it is now. And more often than not we live our lives unconsciously referring to our past experiences as a way to navigate the present.

So the next time you have an argument with someone else, don't assume you know exactly what they think and feel, and don't expect them to know exactly what you think and feel, because it's rarely ever possible. Instead, focus on revisiting the things that shaped you when you were young, and decide whether you want to hold on to those things, or let them go.

**For the next twenty-one days, take a moment to repeat this sentence out loud or in your head. **

"I am more than the things that shaped me."

Chapter Three: Early Learning

Imagine that a painter grows up learning as much as possible about painting. Then she practices, and practices, and becomes excellent.

Now imagine a successful surgeon. She grows up wondering how the human body works, completes medical school and becomes a world class surgeon.

Even though these two women are both successful in their respective careers, the ways of thinking they were trained in are very different.

The painter may rely greatly on creative inspiration to start a masterpiece, whereas the surgeon relies more heavily on principles and known methods to begin performing surgery.

Even though one mode of operation is sometimes seen as superior to the other, this example shows that either way can result in success. It also shows that what we learn in our early years establishes how we continue to learn, and what we may choose to ignore.

For example, after their interests and abilities were observed, the artist may have been encouraged to keep using her imagination, and the surgeon encouraged to keep thinking with sound reasoning, and they may not have found much value in each other's way of thinking.

Since this book is about relationships, an important question to consider is, if childhood education is so fundamental, what did we learn about other people?

The truth is we all have assumptions about others that have been there since childhood, and these assumptions dictate how we continue to learn about other people. So if we learned about people that were very similar to us, maybe we continued to learn along those same lines, not giving thought to people who might have been different from us.

So in the same way the painter was encouraged to develop her imagination to become a great painter, we may have been encouraged to spend our time with friends who had similar interests and abilities, to help with our personal growth.

The point is, while intentions toward perfection are good, too much exclusiveness can limit our understanding of anyone different, and prevent us from having great relationships.

Let's grow in our knowledge of different people.

**For the next twenty-one days, take a moment to repeat this sentence out loud or in your head. **

"I am interested in getting to know people who are different from me."

Chapter Four: Difference.

Whenever you say how you think and feel about something, you are giving people the opportunity to know you. And that's a wonderful thing.

But suppose you were to do this in a discussion, and someone stated a different perspective, how would you feel? Sometimes, no matter how polite or well intentioned someone may be in this situation, you could end up feeling attacked.

Since it's been established that our physical appearance, the environment we grew up in, and what we've learned make us different from each other, it makes sense that we see things differently, and therefore have formed different opinions about everything.

The Beauty of Difference

And one of the biggest reasons we may feel attacked when someone states a different opinion is because we haven't come to terms with difference, and therefore only see its negative effects.

It could help to ask the question, "Why are people different?" Are there any good reasons for that?

The answer is yes! We learn new things that we may have never learned if we hadn't looked at things from someone else's point of view.

But what about moral differences, how could there be good reasons for that?

It can be a terrible feeling to know that on what you consider a serious moral issue, a close friend has a completely different viewpoint from yours. You may ask yourself, can we live with is? Is it even possible?

When a child gets in trouble with their parents, but receives a far less severe punishment than they expected, they feel a great deal of love. Similarly, when you love someone in spite of moral differences, they feel a great deal of love as well, because where judgment was expected, love was received instead.

And isn't it obvious that there's more value in showing a simple act of kindness to someone who is very different from you than in showing it to your best friend?

I think that's a good reason for a moral difference.

**For the next twenty-one days, take a moment to repeat this sentence out loud or in your head. **

"I am kind to everyone, even if they disagree with me."

Chapter Five: Better or worse

What are some differences between you and those closest to you? How do those differences make you feel? Do you appreciate the differences your friends have, or do you decide you are better or worse than them? It's easy to make self-evaluations based on the differences we see in each other.

Whenever we do this, we place barriers in the midst of our relationships. For example, if we were to value ourselves as worse than others because of a difference, we would also try to make up for our imagined shortcoming. This may present itself in the form of putting other people down, or trying to measure up. These actions may be done subtly, or even unconsciously, but they definitely affect our relationships.

In contrast, when we value ourselves as better than others, our focus is on their flaws, and when we continually focus on a person's flaws, that person starts to look like a nuisance, someone we could do without.

Take a moment to think about your closest friends and family. When you notice things you admire about them, do you tell them? And what about their shortcomings, how do you feel about these?

It's important to remember we all have strengths and weaknesses, and that these traits complement each other.

**For the next twenty-one days, take a moment to repeat this sentence out loud or in your head. **

"I am worth the same as everyone else"

Chapter Six: Becoming Enemies

No one likes to think of themselves as having enemies but the truth is we all do. Because whenever we see things differently from each other, and can't be at peace with that, we slowly begin to dislike each other, and with enough time, we become enemies.

Even though no one actually wants enemies, at times, it seems like some people are out to fight wherever they go. This can sometimes be because they have been neglected in the past, and therefore try to prove their importance with any chance they get.

Do you have enemies? What happened to cause that? When answering this question, it's easy to immediately think of the point of escalated conflict that resulted in your separation. Maybe there was a heavy exchange of destructive words, or maybe there was silence where there really needed to be support. Regardless of how it happened, that defining moment which led to the decision to go separate ways is always preceded by the introduction of difference.

When this difference is introduced, sometimes people acknowledge it and try to get rid of it, and other times people ignore it and pretend it isn't there. In either case, the road to enmity begins. And while the point of escalated conflict is usually a long time in the making, some enemies are made a lot quicker than others.

For example, if you not only hate loud music, but that other people listen to it, and were to be stuck in a car with a new co-worker who happened to love loud music, you could reach that point of escalated conflict a lot quicker.

The Beauty of Difference

We all have things we don't like, but should we dislike people because of those things? What would happen if we accepted that it was okay to like different things, how would that affect our relationships?

**For the next twenty-one days, take a moment to repeat this sentence out loud or in your head. **

"I am a friend to all, even if they are my enemy."

Chapter Seven: Difference is okay

<u>The first step</u> we can take to have better relationships is to acknowledge that it's okay to be different. Look around outside! It's easy to see variety and difference everywhere. There are different plants, flowers, and trees. There are also different kinds of buildings everywhere. How boring would it be if there was only one kind of everything?

1. *Let your first goal be to recognize the difference that exists everywhere.*

<u>The second step</u> we can take is to simply be ourselves. We have all learned from different experiences in life, so we can be influential in ways others can't. But sometimes we hide good things about ourselves that could help others, just

so we can fit in. Let's be ourselves, and be good, because someone could benefit from it.

2. *Let your second goal be to stay true to yourself even if you won't fit in.*

<u>The third step</u> we can take is to love. It's the glue that keeps all relationships together.

But what is love?

Simply put, love is treating others the way we want to be treated.

But this definition sometimes raises the question, "how does the idea of discipline or "tough love" fit in with treating others as we want to be treated?"

Discipline or tough love helps change some of our bad behaviors. But when it's given, it's the gentler side of love such as showing kindness or being patient that help assure love's presence.

And by doing this, we are treating others as we want to be treated.

3. *Let your third goal be to show equal amounts of "gentle love", whenever you have to give "tough love."*

Sometimes love is mistaken for "being in love". However "being in love" is a feeling that takes over us, and shifts us from our natural tendency of self-centeredness, to being almost entirely consumed with thoughts about another person. This experience is a freebie from which we can refer to after the magical feelings are gone and we need to exercise our will to love.

**For the next twenty-one days, take a moment to repeat this sentence out loud or in your head. **

"I am changing for the better, one step at a time."

Chapter Eight: Love Training

Practice makes perfect, and pushing through resistance makes us stronger.

Think about the relationships many siblings have. When differences appear between them and conflict arises, they don't have the "luxury" of avoidance that some of us grow accustomed to when we get older. No. Siblings fight, and they fight because they don't have the opportunity to flee.

What a terrible thing we might think it is, to be caged up with people who have different opinions from us. But is it? It seems that the benefit of having to see our siblings again after every fight was that it encouraged us to make peace somehow. Think about all those years of practice and resistance, is it any wonder that some of the best relationships are between siblings?

Take a moment to imagine building and maintaining relationships as a competitive sport in the Olympics. Do you consider yourself ready to qualify, or do you have a lot of training to do? It may be an uncomfortable start, but practice makes perfect, especially with love.

And yes it's true that some people can be very difficult to love. But what if they were part of our training?

What if we could become better at having great relationships because of how we handle the worst people in our lives right now?

Wanna know a secret?...you can.

The secret to great relationships is:

"The Beauty of Difference"

…and the beauty of difference is *love.*

So go ahead, there is no better time than now.

*For the next twenty-one days, take a moment to repeat this sentence out loud or in your head.

"I am at liberty to love."

Thank you for reading!

If this book speaks to you, keep a copy for yourself, re-read it from time to time, and purchase a copy for friends and family

Because with YOUR help, we can encourage the beauty of difference and strengthen relationships all across the world!

About the Author.

Having lived in three different countries before turning thirty, Jon has learned a lot from being around many different people groups. He moved from South Africa, to Ghana, to many places in the United States, and has always been amused by cultural similarities and differences. It's one of his goals to use his unique experience to share something of value with the world.

www.ingramcontent.com/pod-product-compliance
Lightning Source LLC
Chambersburg PA
CBHW031509040426
42444CB00007B/1270